Wheatgrass

A Simple Beginner's Guide to Growing and Juicing, with a 7-Day Starter Plan

copyright © 2025 Felicity Paulman

All rights reserved No part of this book may be reproduced, or stored in a retrieval system, or transmitted in any form or by any means, electronic, mechanical, photocopying, recording, or otherwise, without express written permission of the publisher.

Disclaimer

By reading this disclaimer, you are accepting the terms of the disclaimer in full. If you disagree with this disclaimer, please do not read the guide.

All of the content within this guide is provided for informational and educational purposes only, and should not be accepted as independent medical or other professional advice. The author is not a doctor, physician, nurse, mental health provider, or registered nutritionist/dietician. Therefore, using and reading this guide does not establish any form of a physician-patient relationship.

Always consult with a physician or another qualified health provider with any issues or questions you might have regarding any sort of medical condition. Do not ever disregard any qualified professional medical advice or delay seeking that advice because of anything you have read in this guide. The information in this guide is not intended to be any sort of medical advice and should not be used in lieu of any medical advice by a licensed and qualified medical professional.

The information in this guide has been compiled from a variety of known sources. However, the author cannot attest to or guarantee the accuracy of each source and thus should not be held liable for any errors or omissions.

You acknowledge that the publisher of this guide will not be held liable for any loss or damage of any kind incurred as a result of this guide or the reliance on any information provided within this guide. You acknowledge and agree that you assume all risk and responsibility for any action you undertake in response to the information in this guide.

Using this guide does not guarantee any particular result (e.g., weight loss or a cure). By reading this guide, you acknowledge that there are no guarantees to any specific outcome or results you can expect.

All product names, diet plans, or names used in this guide are for identification purposes only and are the property of their respective owners. The use of these names does not imply endorsement. All other trademarks cited herein are the property of their respective owners.

Where applicable, this guide is not intended to be a substitute for the original work of this diet plan and is, at most, a supplement to the original work for this diet plan and never a direct substitute. This guide is a personal expression of the facts of that diet plan.

Where applicable, persons shown in the cover images are stock photography models and the publisher has obtained the rights to use the images through license agreements with third-party stock image companies.

Table of Contents

Introduction	8
What Is Wheatgrass?	10
A Quick History	10
Why It's Considered a Superfood	12
Nutritional Breakdown	13
Health Benefits of Wheatgrass	18
Detoxification and Liver Support	18
Boosting Immunity and Energy	19
Wheatgrass for Skin, Hair, and Digestion	20
Potential Risks and Who Should Avoid It	21
How to Grow Wheatgrass at Home	23
What You'll Need	23
Step-by-Step Growing Instructions	24
Troubleshooting Common Issues	26
Harvesting Tips	27
How to Juice Wheatgrass	30
Manual vs Electric Juicers	30
Fresh vs Store-Bought Juice	32
Storage Tips for Fresh Juice	34
Daily Usage & Dosage of Wheatgrass	36
How Much to Take and When	36
Wheatgrass Shots vs Smoothie Blends	37
How to Listen to Your Body	39
Wheatgrass Recipes	41
Easy Wheatgrass Smoothies	42
Tropical Wheatgrass Smoothie	43
Berry Blast Smoothie	44
Green Detox Shots	45
Classic Green Detox Shot	46

Apple-Ginger Detox Shot	47
Energy-Boosting Blends	48
Green Superfood Shake	49
Nutty Banana Energy Blend	50
Creative Add-ins	51
Wheatgrass in Everyday Life	**53**
How to Build a Daily Routine Around It	53
Combining Wheatgrass with Other Superfoods	55
Wheatgrass for Kids and Pets	56
Your 7-Day Wheatgrass Starter Plan	**59**
How to Use This Plan	59
Preparing for the Week	60
Daily Routine Overview	62
When to Take Wheatgrass	67
How Much to Start With (and How to Titrate Up)	68
Journaling How You Feel	68
Meal Planning Around Wheatgrass	**70**
Light, Digestive-Friendly Meals	70
Hydration Tips	72
What to Avoid While Detoxing	73
Wheatgrass Detox Side Effects (and How to Manage Them)	**75**
Common Reactions to Wheatgrass Detox	75
What's Normal vs. What's Not	76
Tips to Ease Detox Symptoms	77
7-Day Day-by-Day Plan for Wheatgrass Detox	**79**
Day 1: Introduction & First Shot	79
Day 2: Adding a Second Daily Serving	80
Day 3: Incorporating into a Smoothie	80
Day 4: Tracking Energy & Digestion	81
Day 5: Trying a New Recipe	81
Day 6: Reflecting on Changes	81

Day 7: Wrap-Up and Next Steps — 82
How to Continue After 7 Days — 84
Building a Long-Term Routine — 84
When to Take Breaks — 86
Listening to Your Body's Feedback — 88
Conclusion — 91
FAQs — 94
References and Helpful Links — 96

Introduction

Wheatgrass has long been lauded as a nutritional superfood, and for good reason. Packed with essential vitamins, minerals, antioxidants, and amino acids, this humble green plant offers an impressive range of health benefits despite its modest appearance.

From supporting detoxification and boosting energy to enhancing skin, hair, and digestive health, wheatgrass has earned its place in the wellness world by delivering potent nutrition in every sip, shot, or smoothie.

But wheatgrass is far more than a trendy addition to juice bars or dietary fads. Its roots trace back thousands of years to ancient civilizations that revered it for its rejuvenating properties. Over time, it has evolved from a traditional remedy to a modern superfood backed by scientific studies. For those curious about its history, health advantages, and ways to make it part of daily life, wheatgrass offers an intriguing, nutrient-rich story worth exploring.

In this guide, we will talk about the following:

- What Is Wheatgrass?
- Health Benefits of Wheatgrass
- How to Grow Wheatgrass at Home
- How to Juice Wheatgrass
- Wheatgrass in Everyday Life
- Your 7-Day Wheatgrass Starter Plan
- Meal Planning Around Wheatgrass
- Wheatgrass Detox Side Effects (and How to Manage Them)
- 7-Day Day-by-Day Plan for Wheatgrass Detox
- How to Continue After 7 Days

Keep reading to find out more about this powerful plant and how to incorporate it into your health routine. By the end, you'll not only understand why wheatgrass has become a staple in health-conscious diets, but you'll also walk away with practical tips and creative ideas to make wheatgrass work for your body, schedule, and taste preferences.

What Is Wheatgrass?

Wheatgrass is more than just a trendy health product found in juice bars or Instagram-worthy smoothies. These vibrant green shoots of Triticum aestivum (the common wheat plant) are hailed as a simple yet powerful addition to your diet. To appreciate its value, it's important to understand its rich historical roots, what makes it a superfood, and the incredible nutrition it provides.

Below, we'll explore wheatgrass in depth and uncover why it has become such a staple in the world of natural health.

A Quick History

Although wheatgrass may seem like a modern invention, it's actually been consumed for millennia. Its history spans ancient cultures and modern wellness movements, making it a food with both timeless value and contemporary appeal.

Ancient Beginnings

Wheatgrass traces its origins to ancient civilization, with evidence suggesting that the Ancient Egyptians were among the first to use it. They considered wheatgrass to be a source of vitality and rejuvenation, often associating it with maintaining youthfulness and good health. Historical records indicate that pharaohs and their families consumed wheatgrass juice regularly, believing it strengthened the body and increased energy levels.

Similarly, in parts of Asia and Europe, early communities identified medicinal properties in young wheat plants. It was ground fresh, turned into powders, or infused in teas, allowing the liquid concentrate to act as a tonic for common ailments. Over time, wheatgrass earned a respected place among these ancient remedies.

The Modern Discovery

Wheatgrass gained its modern resurgence in the early 20th century, thanks to a Kansas agricultural chemist named Dr. Charles F. Schnabel. During the 1930s, he noticed how adding wheatgrass to livestock feed dramatically improved the animals' health, resilience, and fertility rates. Fascinated, Dr. Schnabel tested wheatgrass on humans and found similarly positive effects.

By the 1940s, powdered wheatgrass started gaining traction as a health supplement. From improved digestion to enhanced immunity, it became widely recognized as a healing agent. This momentum eventually laid the framework for the wheatgrass juice trend, which began surfacing in the U.S.

during the 1960s, fueled by the growing health-food movement.

Why It's Considered a Superfood

Some foods are labeled as "superfoods" because they're nutrient-dense powerhouses that provide extraordinary health benefits compared to their modest size or calorie count. Wheatgrass is a shining example. Its unique combination of nutrients and compounds has led to widespread recognition as a holistic health booster.

Nutrient Synergy

What truly sets wheatgrass apart is not just the presence of specific vitamins, minerals, or amino acids, but how these elements work together in your body. The synergy of nutrients makes wheatgrass a complete package for improving overall well-being. For example, chlorophyll detoxifies and aids oxygenation, which in turn boosts overall energy levels and cellular function, while antioxidants enhance immunity by reducing oxidative stress.

Raw, Natural, and Unprocessed

One of the reasons wheatgrass is highlighted in clean-eating circles is that it's consumed in its raw form, typically juiced or blended fresh. Unlike many other plants or superfoods that lose nutrients due to cooking or processing, wheatgrass retains its full potency when prepared raw. This makes it a particularly efficient way to deliver bioavailable nutrients to your system.

Versatility

Wheatgrass's superfood qualities also lie in its adaptability. With practically no sugar and negligible calories, it's appropriate for a wide variety of diets, including vegan, paleo, low-carb, and gluten-free eating plans. It's a fantastic option for those dealing with specific dietary restrictions who still want to optimize their nutrition.

Scientifically Supported

Modern studies have also backed the health-supportive claims surrounding wheatgrass. Research has linked wheatgrass to improvements in antioxidant activity, detoxification, immune regulation, and digestive health. While its benefits are substantial, it is important to have realistic expectations and combine wheatgrass with a well-rounded diet to maximize results.

By earning its reputation in both ancient tradition and modern science, wheatgrass has firmly established itself as a superfood that's here to stay.

Nutritional Breakdown

Wheatgrass proves that big benefits can come in small packages. Despite its tiny size, it's loaded with nutrition that can elevate your overall health. Here's a closer look at what's inside every shot of wheatgrass juice.

1. **Key Vitamins**
   - *Vitamin A (as beta-carotene)*: Essential for healthy vision, immune function, and cell growth. Wheatgrass provides a natural source that's easily absorbed by the body.
   - *Vitamin C*: Known for its immune-boosting and antioxidant properties, vitamin C helps protect cells and maintain skin health.
   - *Vitamin E*: Supports skin elasticity, reduces inflammation, and protects cells from damage caused by free radicals.
   - *Vitamin K*: Plays a critical role in blood clotting and bone health.
2. **Minerals**

   Fresh wheatgrass is a natural treasure trove of essential minerals:
   - *Iron*: Vital for oxygen transport in the blood and preventing fatigue.
   - *Magnesium*: Regulates muscle function, nerve signaling, and energy production.
   - *Calcium*: Supports bone density and healthy teeth.
   - *Potassium*: Balances electrolytes and lowers blood pressure.

- ***Selenium and Zinc***: Strengthen immunity, assist metabolic activity, and act as antioxidant catalysts.

3. **Chlorophyll**

   Chlorophyll is the compound that gives wheatgrass its vibrant green color. It's often referred to as "liquid sunshine" because of its ability to detox the body, purify the blood, and aid oxygenation of cells. Chlorophyll is also known to speed healing and promote tissue repair.

4. **Antioxidants**

   Wheatgrass is rich in several antioxidants, including flavonoids and phenolic acids, which protect the body from harmful free radicals. This makes it effective at diminishing cellular damage and reducing the risk of chronic diseases.

5. **Amino Acids**

   Wheatgrass contains 17 amino acids, including all nine essential amino acids that are required for various bodily processes such as protein synthesis and muscle repair.

6. **Enzymes**

   The natural enzymes in wheatgrass, such as protease and amylase, support digestion by breaking down food into absorbable nutrients. They're also thought to help improve metabolic activity, leading to better energy utilization.

7. **Low Calories, Dense Nutrition**

   One of wheatgrass's key advantages is its nutrient-to-calorie ratio. A one-ounce shot of wheatgrass contains just 10-15 calories but delivers a significant dose of beneficial compounds. This makes it ideal for those looking to improve health while maintaining a low-calorie diet.

Though the list above covers many of the main benefits, it's worth noting that wheatgrass also contains trace amounts of rare, beneficial compounds like alkaloids and phytonutrients that improve health on a cellular level.

By incorporating wheatgrass into your day, you're gaining access to an impressive nutritional powerhouse, all delivered in an easily digestible form.

Wheatgrass is more than just a trendy superfood; it's a nutrient-dense gift from nature with a rich history and undeniable benefits. Ancient Egyptians knew of its value, modern science supports its incredible health properties, and its impressive nutritional profile continues to set it apart.

Whether you grow your own wheatgrass at home, incorporate it into a smoothie, or sip on a fresh shot at your favorite juice bar, this simple green plant has the potential to make a big impact on your overall well-being. Understanding what wheatgrass is, where it comes from, and why it's so celebrated is the first step in unveiling all it has to offer.

Health Benefits of Wheatgrass

Wheatgrass isn't just a health trend; it's a nutrient-packed superfood that can positively impact many aspects of your health when consumed regularly. It helps detox your body, boosts immunity, improves your energy levels, and even enhances the look and feel of your skin and hair. Like all health supplements, though, it comes with some precautions. Let's break it down in simple terms.

Detoxification and Liver Support

Detoxing might sound like a trendy word, but the idea is straightforward. Your body is constantly working to flush out toxins from food, water, and the environment. Wheatgrass helps support this process, especially through the liver, which is the body's main filtering system.

- **How It Works**: Wheatgrass is loaded with chlorophyll, the green plant pigment often called "nature's detoxifier." Chlorophyll aids the liver by filtering out harmful substances from the blood. It also helps bind toxins in the digestive system, so your body can get rid of them more effectively.

- ***Benefits for Your Liver***: A healthy liver is crucial for energy, digestion, and even hormonal balance. Wheatgrass helps reduce the strain on your liver by giving it the tools it needs to work more efficiently.

Practical Tip: Start your day with a shot of fresh wheatgrass juice to kickstart the detoxifying process. Drink water throughout the day to help flush those toxins out.

Boosting Immunity and Energy

Wheatgrass is like a spark plug for your immune system and energy levels. Packed with vitamins, antioxidants, and minerals, it helps your body stay strong and active.

- ***Immune Booster***: Wheatgrass is rich in vitamin C and zinc, both of which help your immune system fight off colds, infections, and other illnesses. The antioxidants in wheatgrass also protect your cells from damage caused by free radicals, which can weaken immunity over time.
- ***Energy Enhancer***: Feeling sluggish? The high levels of chlorophyll in wheatgrass help oxygenate the blood, improving circulation and energizing your cells. This can make you feel more awake and alert naturally, without relying on caffeine.

Practical Tip: If you struggle with the afternoon energy slump, try adding a wheatgrass shot to your afternoon routine instead of reaching for a sugary snack or coffee.

Wheatgrass for Skin, Hair, and Digestion

Wheatgrass isn't just good for what's happening inside your body; it can also improve your outward appearance and digestion.

- *Clearer Skin*: The antioxidants and chlorophyll in wheatgrass help combat inflammation, reduce redness, and promote clear skin. Plus, it supports healthy cell renewal, which is essential for glowing skin.
- *Healthier Hair*: Wheatgrass has iron, magnesium, and vitamins like A and E, all of which are crucial for strong, healthy hair. Regularly consuming wheatgrass may reduce hair thinning and promote shiny, resilient strands.
- *Better Digestion*: If you're often bloated or feel heavy after meals, wheatgrass may help. It contains natural enzymes that aid digestion by breaking down food more efficiently. Its fiber content can also support gut health and regular bowel movements.

Practical Tips:

- Apply a wheatgrass paste or cream (made from powdered wheatgrass and water) directly to your skin to help with blemishes and irritation.
- Try adding powdered wheatgrass to your morning smoothie for digestive support.

Potential Risks and Who Should Avoid It

Even though wheatgrass is a natural and nutritious superfood, it might not be suitable for everyone. Here are some things to keep in mind:

- *Allergic Reactions*: Some people may have an allergy to wheatgrass, especially if they are sensitive to grasses or pollen. If you notice itching, hives, or difficulty breathing after consuming wheatgrass, stop immediately and see a doctor.
- *Upset Stomach*: For beginners, wheatgrass can sometimes cause nausea or diarrhea as your body adjusts. Start with a small dose (like half an ounce) and gradually increase it.
- *Gluten Concerns*: While wheatgrass itself doesn't contain gluten, traces from the wheat plant could contaminate it. If you have celiac disease or a severe gluten sensitivity, ensure you're purchasing certified gluten-free wheatgrass products.
- *Pregnant or Breastfeeding Women*: There's limited research on wheatgrass for those who are pregnant or

nursing, so it's a good idea to check with your doctor before starting.

Practical Tip: Always buy wheatgrass from a trusted source. If it's grown in non-sterile conditions, there's a chance it could be contaminated with harmful bacteria.

Wheatgrass can be a fantastic addition to your wellness routine. It helps detox your body, supports your immune system, energizes you, and boosts your skin, hair, and digestion. However, you should start slow, watch for any adverse reactions, and ensure that it's right for your body and lifestyle.

How to Grow Wheatgrass at Home

Growing wheatgrass at home is simple, cost-effective, and incredibly rewarding. With just a small space and a few basic materials, you'll have a fresh supply of nutrient-packed wheatgrass in as little as a week. Here's your step-by-step guide to get started!

What You'll Need

Before you begin, gather these essential materials to ensure a smooth growing process:

1. ***Wheatgrass Seeds*** (also known as wheat berries): Organic, untreated seeds work best. You can find them online or at health food stores.
2. ***Growing Tray***: A shallow plastic or metal tray, ideally about 1–2 inches deep, with holes for drainage. You can repurpose old baking trays or storage containers, as long as they allow water to drain.
3. ***Potting Soil or Growing Medium***:
    - Potting soil is the most common and effective.
    - Coconut coir or seed-starting mix can also be used as a soil alternative.

4. ***Spray Bottle***: For misting the seeds and keeping the soil evenly moist.
5. ***Drainage Plate or Mat*** (optional): Placed under your trays to catch any excess water.
6. ***Water***: Clean, filtered water is recommended for optimal growth.
7. ***Sunlight or Grow Light***:
   - A windowsill with indirect sunlight works well.
   - If natural light isn't available, use LED or fluorescent grow lights.

Practical Tip: Many stores sell complete wheatgrass growing kits that include seeds, trays, and all necessary supplies. These can be helpful if you're just starting out.

Step-by-Step Growing Instructions

Follow these steps to grow your wheatgrass successfully:

Step 1: Prepare the Seeds

- Measure about 1 cup of wheatgrass seeds. This is sufficient for one standard-sized growing tray.
- Rinse your seeds thoroughly in cold water to remove any dirt or debris.
- Place the seeds in a clean bowl and cover them with water. They should soak for 8–12 hours (overnight is ideal). This softens the seeds and speeds up germination.

- After soaking, drain the seeds and rinse them again. Spread them out on a clean surface or keep them in a strainer for another 12 hours to begin sprouting.

Step 2: Prepare the Tray

- Fill your tray with about 1 inch of potting soil or growing medium. Spread it evenly, but don't pack it too tightly.
- Water the soil lightly. It should feel damp, like a wrung-out sponge, but not soggy.

Step 3: Spread the Seeds

- Evenly distribute your sprouted seeds across the surface of the soil. They should form a single layer and touch each other, but not overlap too much.
- Lightly press the seeds into the soil, ensuring good contact. Avoid burying them.

Step 4: Cover and Water

- Gently mist the seeds with a spray bottle to keep them moist.
- Cover the tray with another shallow tray or a clean kitchen towel for the first two days. This creates a dark, humid environment that encourages sprouting and reduces evaporation.
- Check and spray the seeds daily to prevent them from drying out.

Step 5: Uncover and Grow

- After 2–3 days, remove the cover once you see small sprouts emerging. Place the tray in a location with indirect sunlight or under a grow light for 4–6 hours per day.
- Continue misting the shoots twice a day to keep them hydrated, but avoid over-soaking the soil as it may cause mold.

Step 6: Growth Period:

Over the next week, your wheatgrass will grow rapidly, reaching about 6–10 inches tall. Keep the soil moist but not flooded, and check for any issues like mold or pests.

<u>**Practical Tip**</u>:

If you're growing several trays, stagger planting them by a couple of days to ensure you always have a fresh batch ready to harvest.

Troubleshooting Common Issues

Sometimes, things don't go as planned. Here are some common problems and how to fix them:

1. **Mold Growth:**
   - Causes: Overwatering or poor ventilation.
   - Solution: Reduce humidity by watering less frequently and adding a fan for airflow. If mold

appears, spray the affected area lightly with a water and vinegar solution (3 parts water, 1 part vinegar).

2. **Seeds Don't Sprout:**
   - Causes: Old or poor-quality seeds.
   - Solution: Ensure your seeds are fresh, organic, and untreated.
3. **Yellow Wheatgrass:**
   - Causes: Lack of light.
   - Solution: Move the tray to a brighter location or provide more exposure to natural or artificial light.
4. **Uneven Growth:**
   - Causes: Uneven seed distribution or water coverage.
   - Solution: Ensure the seeds are spread evenly over the soil and watered uniformly.

<u>**Practical Tip**</u>: Keep your growing area clean and avoid overcrowding trays, as this can lead to poor ventilation and increase the risk of mold.

Harvesting Tips

Harvesting is the most exciting part of the process! Follow these simple tips for the best results:

1. **When to Harvest:**
   - Wheatgrass is ready to harvest once it reaches about 6–8 inches tall (this usually takes 7–10 days). The grass will have a vibrant green color and a sweet aroma.
   - Harvest it promptly, as wheatgrass becomes less flavorful and nutrient-rich once it matures.
2. **How to Harvest:**
   - Use clean scissors or a sharp knife to cut the wheatgrass just above the soil line.
   - Harvest in batches if your tray has uneven growth, or cut all the grass at once if it's uniform.
3. **Storing Freshly Cut Wheatgrass:**

   Wrap the cut wheatgrass in a damp paper towel or store it in an airtight container in the refrigerator. It will stay fresh for up to 7 days.

4. **Multiple Harvests:**

   Wheatgrass can regrow after the first harvest, but subsequent growths tend to be thinner and less flavorful. For the best results, most people replant seeds after the first harvest.

Practical Tip: To avoid waste, only grow as much wheatgrass as you can consume in a week or two.

Growing wheatgrass at home is an easy and rewarding project, even for beginners. With just a little effort, you'll have the freshest, most nutrient-packed wheatgrass to use in juices, smoothies, and recipes. Plus, growing it yourself means you can control the entire process, ensuring your wheatgrass is clean, safe, and free from chemicals.

How to Juice Wheatgrass

Wheatgrass juice is a powerful addition to your health routine, packed with nutrients like chlorophyll, vitamins, and antioxidants. But before you toss a handful of wheatgrass into your blender, it's important to know that juicing wheatgrass requires some specific tools and techniques to get the most out of it. Here's a beginner-friendly guide to help you get started.

Manual vs Electric Juicers

Not all juicers are created equal, especially when it comes to wheatgrass. Because wheatgrass is fibrous and tricky to extract juice from, it requires the right juicing equipment. Here's a breakdown of your options.

Manual Juicers

How They Work: These hand-operated juicers use a handle or crank to press juice from wheatgrass. You feed the grass into the machine, and the crank squeezes out the juice.

Benefits:

- Affordable compared to electric models.
- Compact and easy to store.
- Great for small batches of juice.

Drawbacks:

- Requires effort and time, as you must manually turn the crank.
- Not ideal if you're juicing in large quantities.

Practical Tip: Manual juicers are perfect for beginners or those who want to juice small amounts of wheatgrass occasionally.

Electric Juicers

How They Work: These plug-in machines automate the juicing process, making them quicker and easier to use. Look for masticating (cold-press) juicers, as centrifugal juicers often aren't effective for wheatgrass.

Benefits:

- Effortless and speedy.
- Extracts juice more efficiently, producing a higher yield.
- Suitable for regular juicers who want to make bigger batches.

Drawbacks:

- Pricier than manual juicers.

- Bulkier and requires more countertop or storage space.
- May take longer to clean.

Practical Tip: If you juice wheatgrass often or in larger amounts, investing in an electric masticating juicer is worth it for its convenience and efficiency.

Which Should You Choose?
- If you're just getting started and want something budget-friendly, go for a manual juicer.
- If you're serious about juicing wheatgrass regularly and time is a factor, opt for an electric masticating juicer.

Other Option: If you don't have a juicer and don't mind a bit of effort, you can use a blender and cheesecloth. Blend the wheatgrass with a small amount of water, strain it through the cheesecloth, and squeeze out the juice manually.

Fresh vs Store-Bought Juice

When it comes to enjoying wheatgrass juice, you can choose between making it fresh at home or buying it premade from the store. Both options have their pros and cons.

Fresh Wheatgrass Juice
Benefits:
- Contains the highest amount of nutrients, as it is unprocessed and consumed immediately after juicing.

- You control the quality of the wheatgrass by growing or sourcing it yourself.
- No additives or preservatives.

Drawbacks:

- Takes more effort and time to prepare.
- Requires access to a juicer and fresh wheatgrass.

Practical Tip: Drink fresh wheatgrass juice immediately to ensure you're getting the maximum nutritional value.

Store-Bought Wheatgrass Juice
Benefits:

- Convenient for those who don't have time or tools to juice at home.
- Often comes in single-serving bottles, making it easy to grab and go.

Drawbacks:

- May contain preservatives, reducing its nutritional value.
- Store-bought juice is usually pasteurized, which can further deplete nutrients.
- It can be pricey compared to DIY juicing.

Practical Tip: If you opt for store-bought juice, look for ones labeled "cold-pressed" and "100% wheatgrass juice" for the best quality.

Storage Tips for Fresh Juice

If you've juiced more than you can drink at once, don't worry! Here are some tips to store your wheatgrass juice while preserving its nutrients and flavor.

1. **Use an Airtight Glass Container**
   - Pour the juice into a clean, airtight glass jar or container. Avoid plastic since it can interact with the juice and reduce its quality.
   - Fill the container as much as possible to minimize air exposure, which can speed up nutrient loss.
2. **Refrigerate Immediately**

   Place the container in the fridge right after juicing. Fresh wheatgrass juice can last up to 48 hours when stored properly, but it's best to drink it within 24 hours for maximum benefits.

3. **Freeze for Longer Storage**
   - To extend its shelf life, freeze your wheatgrass juice. Use small portions, such as in ice cube trays, so you can easily thaw the amount you need.
   - Frozen juice can be stored for up to 1 month, though it's best consumed as soon as possible to retain nutrients.

4. **Avoid Heat and Light**

   Heat and sunlight cause nutrients in wheatgrass juice to deteriorate quickly. Store it in a dark, cool place until it's refrigerated or consumed.

Practical Tip: Label your containers with the date of juicing so you know how fresh your juice is and can avoid wasting it.

Juicing wheatgrass might seem like a lot of work at first, but with the right tools and tips, it becomes a simple and rewarding process. Choosing between a manual or electric juicer depends on your needs, and while fresh juice is ideal for the highest nutrients, store-bought options can be a convenient backup. Proper storage is key to getting the most out of your wheatgrass juice, so always keep it airtight, cool, and free from exposure to sunlight.

Daily Usage & Dosage of Wheatgrass

Wheatgrass is a nutrient-packed superfood that can support overall health, boost energy, and aid in detoxifying the body. Whether you're new to wheatgrass or looking to optimize your routine, understanding the right daily dosage and consumption method is key. This guide walks you through how much to take, how to enjoy it best, and how to fine-tune your intake to your body's needs.

How Much to Take and When

For beginners, it's best to start small. The recommended starting dose is 1 ounce (around 30 milliliters) of fresh wheatgrass juice or 1 teaspoon of wheatgrass powder mixed with water. This amount is gentle on your stomach and gives your body time to adjust to its potency.

After 3–5 days, if your body feels comfortable and energized, increase to 2 servings per day. You can take one serving in the morning and another in the early afternoon, but avoid taking wheatgrass too late in the day as it might boost your energy and interfere with sleep.

For regular users or those more experienced with wheatgrass, daily intake can be as much as 2–3 ounces (up to 90 milliliters) of juice, depending on how your body responds. Remember, more is not always better. Overdoing it may lead to discomfort, like nausea or upset stomach.

Key Tips:

- *Morning Boost*: Taking wheatgrass on an empty stomach first thing in the morning maximizes its nutrient absorption.
- *Hydration First*: Drink a glass of water 20–30 minutes beforehand to hydrate your system and improve digestion.
- *Pre-Meal Timing*: Consuming wheatgrass 30 minutes before meals can help stimulate digestion.

Wheatgrass Shots vs Smoothie Blends

In this section, we will discuss the difference between wheatgrass shots and smoothie blends. Both are popular ways of consuming wheatgrass, but they have distinct differences in terms of preparation and benefits.

Wheatgrass Shots

Wheatgrass shots are a straightforward and quick way to consume this superfood. They deliver a concentrated dose of nutrients in one small serving, making them ideal for busy mornings. Shots are best taken on their own, followed by a glass of water to cleanse the palate and aid absorption.

Benefits:

- Quick and easy to prepare.
- Delivers a strong dosage without additional ingredients.
- Perfect for individuals who prefer simplicity.

The taste of pure wheatgrass juice is earthy and can be too strong for some. It may take a few tries to get used to its flavor.

Smoothie Blends

For those who dislike the robust taste of wheatgrass juice, blending it into a smoothie is a great alternative. Smoothies allow you to mask the taste while adding extra nutrients from fruits, vegetables, and plant-based milk.

For example, mix 1 teaspoon of wheatgrass powder or 1 ounce of juice with spinach, a ripe banana, frozen berries, and almond milk for a delicious, nutrient-dense drink. Smoothies are also an excellent meal replacement or snack option during the day.

Benefits:

- Tastes better when paired with fruits and other ingredients.
- More satisfying and filling than a shot.
- Allows for creative combinations that support balanced nutrition.

Be mindful of smoothie ingredients. Avoid adding too much sugar, such as from sweetened yogurts or juices, as this could counteract wheatgrass's detoxifying properties.

How to Listen to Your Body

When incorporating wheatgrass into your routine, it's important to pay attention to how your body responds. People react differently depending on their body type, diet, and pre-existing health conditions.

- *Energy Levels*: Increased energy is a common sign that wheatgrass is working for you. If you feel sluggish or overly fatigued, reduce the dose and monitor the effects.
- *Digestion*: Wheatgrass can promote regular digestion, but some people may experience initial bloating or an upset stomach. These symptoms typically resolve as your body adjusts. If discomfort lasts more than a few days, lower your intake or consult a healthcare provider.
- *Detox Symptoms*: Mild headaches or nausea are normal during the early stages of consumption as the

body releases toxins. Stay hydrated and eat light meals to help ease these reactions.
- **Overall Well-Being**: If you feel good, that's your sign to maintain or slightly increase your intake. If you feel unwell, dial back and reassess.

Tips for Adjusting Dosage:

- Start small and gradually increase to find your personal "sweet spot."
- Take breaks if you notice prolonged side effects or detox symptoms.
- Every few weeks, skip wheatgrass for a few days to give your body a rest and prevent over-dependence.

Wheatgrass is a versatile superfood with numerous health benefits when used correctly. Whether you prefer to take it quickly as a shot or incorporate it into a nutritious smoothie, the key is finding what works best for your body and schedule. Start with the recommended dosage, listen to how your body responds, and adjust accordingly. With consistent use and a mindful approach, wheatgrass can become an enjoyable and beneficial part of your daily health routine.

Wheatgrass Recipes

In this chapter, we'll provide some delicious and easy-to-make recipes that incorporate wheatgrass. These recipes are not only nutritious but also taste great, making it easier to incorporate wheatgrass into your diet.

Easy Wheatgrass Smoothies

Smoothies are the perfect vehicle for wheatgrass, allowing you to blend its bold flavor with naturally sweet and creamy ingredients for a balanced, delicious drink.

Tropical Wheatgrass Smoothie

Ingredients:

- 1 ounce (2 tablespoons) wheatgrass juice or 1 teaspoon wheatgrass powder
- 1 frozen banana
- ½ cup pineapple chunks
- ½ cup unsweetened coconut water
- 1 tablespoon chia seeds (optional)
- A squeeze of fresh lime juice

Instructions:

1. Add all the ingredients to a blender.
2. Blend on high until smooth. Add a splash of water if the consistency is too thick.
3. Pour into a glass and enjoy your tropical, nutrient-packed treat!

Berry Blast Smoothie

Ingredients:

- 1 ounce wheatgrass juice or 1 teaspoon powdered wheatgrass
- ½ cup mixed berries (strawberries, blueberries, raspberries)
- ½ cup unsweetened almond milk (or any milk of your choice)
- 1 tablespoon almond butter
- 1 teaspoon honey or maple syrup (optional)

Instructions:

1. Combine all the ingredients in a blender.
2. Blend until smooth and creamy.
3. Serve chilled for a refreshing and antioxidant-rich drink.

Tip: To mask the flavor of wheatgrass in smoothies, pair it with sweet fruits like banana, mango, or berries. They neutralize its earthy taste while adding natural sweetness.

Green Detox Shots

Wheatgrass's natural detoxifying properties make it an ideal choice for health shots. These tiny doses of green power are quick, potent, and perfect for starting your day.

Classic Green Detox Shot

Ingredients:

- 1 ounce freshly juiced wheatgrass
- Juice of ½ a lemon
- Pinch of cayenne pepper (optional)

Instructions:

1. Mix the wheatgrass juice and lemon juice in a small glass.
2. Sprinkle a tiny pinch of cayenne if you want an added metabolism boost.
3. Drink it in one swift sip!

Apple-Ginger Detox Shot

Ingredients:

- 1 ounce wheatgrass juice or 1 teaspoon powdered wheatgrass mixed with water
- Juice of ½ a green apple
- ½ teaspoon grated ginger

Instructions:

1. Mix wheatgrass juice, apple juice, and ginger in a shot glass.
2. Stir well and drink fresh.

Tip: If the grassy flavor feels too strong, chase your detox shot with a slice of orange or a sip of water to cleanse your palate.

Energy-Boosting Blends

For a natural pick-me-up during busy days, wheatgrass blends are a game-changer. They combine the goodness of wheatgrass with energy-supporting ingredients like nuts, seeds, and superfoods.

Green Superfood Shake

Ingredients:

- 1 ounce wheatgrass juice
- 1 handful fresh spinach
- 1 cup unsweetened almond milk
- 1 tablespoon rolled oats
- 1 tablespoon flaxseed
- 1 teaspoon matcha powder (optional)

Instructions:

1. Add all the ingredients to a blender.
2. Blend until smooth and creamy.
3. Pour into a travel-friendly bottle for an on-the-go energy boost.

Nutty Banana Energy Blend

Ingredients:

- 1 ounce wheatgrass juice or 1 teaspoon wheatgrass powder
- 1 ripe banana
- 1 cup unsweetened oat milk
- 1 tablespoon peanut or almond butter
- ½ teaspoon cinnamon

Instructions:

1. Combine everything in a blender and blend until smooth.
2. Serve immediately, garnished with a sprinkle of cinnamon.

Tip: For an extra energy kick, add a scoop of protein powder or a tablespoon of cacao nibs to your blends.

Creative Add-ins

Sometimes the right add-ins can turn wheatgrass recipes into something truly special. Here are some simple yet impactful ingredients to pair with wheatgrass and how to use them:

- *Lemon*: Bright and tangy, lemon juice complements the grassy flavor of wheatgrass beautifully. Try adding it to shots or smoothies for a zesty twist. For example, a squeeze of lemon in your detox shot can boost its alkalizing effects.
- *Mint*: Fresh mint leaves bring a cooling note to wheatgrass recipes. Blend a few leaves into your smoothies or garnish your wheatgrass shots to elevate the flavor.
- *Ginger*: Spicy and warming, ginger pairs wonderfully with wheatgrass. Add a small piece of fresh ginger to your smoothies or grate it into your detox shot for extra zing.
- *Apple*: Sweet and crisp, apple cuts through the earthy notes of wheatgrass. Juice it, blend it, or chop it finely as a topping for smoothie bowls.

Pro Tip: Don't be afraid to experiment with combinations. A wheatgrass smoothie with mint, mango, and lime makes a tropical delight, while ginger, apple, and spinach create a grounding green drink.

Wheatgrass is an incredibly versatile ingredient that can fit seamlessly into various recipes. Whether you prefer quick detox shots, energy-loaded blends, or sweet and fruity smoothies, there's a wheatgrass recipe for every mood and occasion.

Wheatgrass in Everyday Life

Wheatgrass is a versatile superfood that can be easily incorporated into your daily life, benefiting not just you but your family—including kids and pets. Below, we provide practical tips to help you make wheatgrass an effortless part of your routine.

How to Build a Daily Routine Around It

Consistency is key for reaping the health benefits of wheatgrass, and building a daily habit can be surprisingly easy. Here's how to make it work for you:

1. **Start Your Morning with Wheatgrass**

    Kick off your day with a shot of wheatgrass or a wheatgrass-enhanced smoothie. Drinking it on an empty stomach allows your body to absorb the nutrients more effectively. For a quick morning routine:

    - Juice your wheatgrass the night before and store it in an airtight container in the fridge.

- Pair it with a wedge of lemon or orange to chase its earthy flavor.
- Combine it with other morning superfoods like chia pudding or overnight oats.

2. **Use It During Midday Slumps**

If you find your energy dipping in the afternoon, wheatgrass can provide a natural pick-me-up. Opt for:

- A mid-afternoon wheatgrass shot to refresh and energize you.
- A smoothie with wheatgrass, fresh fruit, and a handful of nuts to power through the rest of the day.

3. **Add It Post-Workout**

Wheatgrass is great for recovery. Its antioxidant and anti-inflammatory properties help combat stress from exercise. Post-workout ideas:

- Blend wheatgrass into a protein shake with almond milk, banana, and a scoop of protein powder.
- Take a wheatgrass shot alongside a small snack like Greek yogurt or a boiled egg.

4. **Evening Rejuvenation**

Wheatgrass's detoxifying benefits align well with a calming evening routine. Sip a light wheatgrass-infused drink as part of your wind-down:

- Stir wheatgrass powder into warm water with a dash of honey for a soothing beverage.
- Pair it with a light, healthy dinner focused on fresh, whole ingredients.

Pro Tip: Set a reminder on your phone or align your wheatgrass ritual with an existing habit, like making coffee or brushing your teeth.

Combining Wheatgrass with Other Superfoods

Wheatgrass works brilliantly alongside other superfoods, enhancing both nutritional value and flavor. Here are some winning combinations:

1. *Matcha*: Both wheatgrass and matcha are rich in antioxidants. Mix wheatgrass into your matcha latte or combine it in a smoothie for a double dose of nutrients and energy.
2. *Chia Seeds*: Chia seeds are high in omega-3 fatty acids and fiber. Create a morning power bowl by blending wheatgrass into your smoothie base and topping it with soaked chia seeds and fresh fruits.
3. *Kale & Spinach*: Pair wheatgrass with these leafy greens in a juice or smoothie for a chlorophyll-rich drink that supports detoxification and boosts iron intake.

4. *Turmeric*: Known for its anti-inflammatory properties, turmeric pairs well with the cleansing power of wheatgrass. Add both to warm water with a pinch of black pepper for an immune-boosting tonic.
5. *Avocado*: For a creamy, nutrient-packed option, blend wheatgrass with avocado, lime, and coconut milk into a refreshing chilled soup or smoothie.

Pro Tip: Don't shy away from experimenting. Superfood blends provide an opportunity to cater to your unique dietary needs while keeping things flavorful and exciting!

Wheatgrass for Kids and Pets

Wheatgrass isn't just for adults. With proper preparation, it can also benefit children and your furry companions. Here's how to make it work for everyone:

Wheatgrass for Kids

While kids might be hesitant to try something so green, there are simple ways to introduce wheatgrass into their diets:

- *Sneak it into Smoothies*: Blend a small amount of wheatgrass juice or powder into a fruit-heavy smoothie filled with strawberries, bananas, or mangoes for a naturally sweet drink.
- *Wheatgrass Ice Pops*: Mix wheatgrass juice with orange juice or apple juice, then freeze into popsicle molds as a fun, nutrient-packed treat.

- *Include it in Sauces*: Add a teaspoon of wheatgrass powder to pasta sauces, soups, or dips, where the flavor can blend in unnoticed.

Tip for Picky Eaters: Keep the portions small when starting out and focus on recipes where wheatgrass isn't the main event.

Wheatgrass for Pets

Pets can benefit from wheatgrass too, thanks to its vitamins, antioxidants, and digestive support properties. Here's how to incorporate it:

- *For Dogs*: Add a teaspoon of wheatgrass powder to their food or mix a small amount of wheatgrass juice into their water (start with diluted juice and increase slowly).
- *For Cats*: Cats naturally enjoy nibbling plants, so a small patch of wheatgrass can double as entertainment and a healthy snack.
- *For Small Animals*: If you own small pets like rabbits or guinea pigs, they'll also enjoy fresh wheatgrass as a supplement to their usual diet.

Safety Note: Always introduce wheatgrass slowly to your pets and monitor their reactions. Consult your veterinarian before making it a staple in their diet.

Pro Tip for Pets: Grow wheatgrass at home to ensure a fresh and organic source for you and your pets. It's a simple and fun project for the family!

Incorporating wheatgrass into your daily routine is simple and rewarding. Add it to your meals, pair it with superfoods, or use creative ways to include it in diets for kids and pets. From wheatgrass shots to blending it into recipes, this superfood supports health and wellness for everyone.

Your 7-Day Wheatgrass Starter Plan

Wheatgrass is a nutritional powerhouse packed with vitamins, antioxidants, and chlorophyll to help you feel energized and refreshed. To make it a consistent part of your routine, a 7-day starter plan is a great way to ease in while exploring how it best fits your lifestyle.

This plan includes everything you need to get started—from prepping your kitchen to daily tips on how to take wheatgrass. Whether you're a beginner or looking for inspiration, this guide will set you on the right path.

How to Use This Plan

This 7-day plan is designed to help you gradually incorporate wheatgrass into your daily life. Starting small and building up is key, as it allows your body to adjust to the superfood's detoxifying properties. Here's how to customize it:

- ***Listen to Your Body***: Everyone is different. If you feel great, you can increase your dosage gradually. If your

body feels overwhelmed, slow down and take smaller doses.
- ***Customize for Your Schedule***: You can adjust the times and preparation methods to suit your routine (e.g., morning energy boost or a midday pick-me-up).
- ***Journal Your Experience***: Use the journaling tips at the end of the plan to track how wheatgrass makes you feel and adjust as needed.

The goal is to establish a routine, try various methods, and discover what works best for your lifestyle.

Preparing for the Week

Getting set up for success starts with preparation. Here are the steps to organize your wheatgrass adventure:

What to Buy

1. **Wheatgrass Options**

   Tip: If you prefer the freshest option, buy or grow fresh wheatgrass at home.

   - Wheatgrass Juice (Fresh or Frozen): Pre-made juice is convenient if you're short on time.
   - Wheatgrass Powder: Great for blending into smoothies or water.

2. **Juicer (Optional)**

   While not absolutely necessary, a masticating juicer is the best tool for fresh wheatgrass juice. Regular blenders or centrifugal juicers don't work well for juicing wheatgrass.

3. **Accessories**
   - Small shot glasses for measuring wheatgrass juice.
   - Reusable ice cube trays (if using frozen juice).
   - A chopping board and a small knife for prepping add-ins like lemon and ginger.

Tips for Prepping Your Kitchen

- ***Designate a Space***: Setting aside a specific spot in your kitchen with all your wheatgrass supplies makes sticking to this habit easier.
- ***Keep Ingredients Handy***: Pre-wash fruits and store them in easy-to-access containers.
- ***Batch Prep***: If using fresh wheatgrass, juice a batch every 2–3 days and store it in an airtight container. Alternatively, portion wheatgrass powder for the week so it's ready to use.

Pro Tip: If you're new to juicing, start with pre-made wheatgrass juice or powder, as it's quicker and easier to incorporate.

Optional Add-ins

Wheatgrass is nutritious on its own, but adding natural flavors can enhance both its taste and health benefits. Here are some popular options to experiment with:

- *Lemon*: Zesty and alkalizing, a squeeze of lemon juice complements wheatgrass well.
- *Ginger*: A spicy kick of ginger boosts digestion and pairs perfectly in smoothies or shots.
- *Apple*: Sweet and crisp, apple juice or slices can balance the grassy flavor of wheatgrass.
- *Mint*: A few fresh mint leaves add a refreshing twist to wheatgrass drinks.

Pro Tip: Rotate your add-ins throughout the week to keep your wheatgrass routine exciting and flavorful.

Daily Routine Overview

Developing a consistent routine is key to integrating wheatgrass into your daily life while maximizing its health benefits. This 7-day plan provides a simple yet flexible structure to help beginners ease into the process without overwhelming their bodies. Below, you'll find a detailed breakdown of each day's steps, along with practical tips and recipe ideas to make your experience enjoyable and rewarding.

Days 1–2: Start Slow, Allow Your Body to Adjust

1. ***Morning Routine***
   - Begin with **half an ounce (15 ml)** of fresh wheatgrass juice or **½ teaspoon** of powdered wheatgrass mixed with water. If the taste feels strong, mix it into a small smoothie or pair it with a wedge of lemon to cut the earthy flavor.
   - If you're feeling adventurous, try it in a simple blend with fresh ginger and an apple slice for added sweetness and zing.
   - It's best to take wheatgrass on an empty stomach in the morning to make sure your body absorbs the nutrients fully.

2. ***Goal for These Days***

   These first couple of days are all about easing your body into the detox process. Wheatgrass's high chlorophyll and antioxidant content might cause mild cleansing symptoms, such as slight headaches or fatigue, but these should pass quickly as your body adjusts. Make sure to drink plenty of water throughout the day to help support the detox.

3. ***Tips for Success***
   - Pair wheatgrass with a small piece of fruit like a banana or an orange slice if the taste is overwhelming.

- If you're using powdered wheatgrass, mix it in cold water or sprinkle it over a bowl of yogurt for variety.

Days 3–4: Gradually Increase Your Dose

1. ***Increasing Intake***
   - Bump up your dosage to **1 ounce (30 ml)** of fresh wheatgrass juice or **1 teaspoon** of powdered wheatgrass.
   - If your body has adjusted well, consider dividing your intake into two sessions per day. Take one dose in the morning and the second in the early afternoon to see the impact on your energy levels.

2. ***Afternoon Experimentation***

   Test how wheatgrass works as a mid-day pick-me-up. Blender enthusiasts can try a refreshing tropical smoothie recipe:

   Blend: 1 teaspoon of wheatgrass, half a frozen banana, a handful of pineapple chunks, spinach, and coconut water.

   This combination masks the taste of wheatgrass while delivering a delicious energy boost packed with vitamins.

3. ***Goal for These Days***

You're now building your body's tolerance to wheatgrass's nutritional effects while finding a schedule that fits your unique lifestyle. Monitor how you feel throughout the day and make adjustments if necessary.

4. ***Tips for Success***
    - For a quick detox kick, create a shot by mixing wheatgrass juice with freshly squeezed ginger juice and a splash of apple juice.
    - Avoid overloading smoothies with excessive fruits or sweeteners; aim to keep them light and nutrient-dense.

Days 5–7: Find Your Groove and Focus on Consistency

1. ***Consistent Intake***
    - Stick with a *1-ounce daily dose* of wheatgrass juice or *1 teaspoon of powder*, splitting into morning and afternoon servings if needed.
    - If you feel ready, you can gradually increase to *2–3 ounces daily* (60–90 ml) for additional benefits, but don't exceed this amount unless it feels comfortable for your body.
2. ***Combine Superfoods***: Amp up your green smoothie by adding other superfoods like chia seeds, lemon juice, kale, or spirulina. For example, try this nutrient-packed blend:

- **Ingredients**: 1 teaspoon wheatgrass, ½ cup frozen mango chunks, a handful of spinach, 1 teaspoon chia seeds, juice from half a lemon, and almond milk.
- **Instructions**: Blend everything together for an energizing and satisfying breakfast or snack.

3. **Adjust for Convenience**
   - If preparing fresh wheatgrass juice feels too time-consuming, switch to high-quality powdered wheatgrass. It's just as effective and far quicker to prepare. Mix it into water, your favorite smoothie, or even herbal tea for a warm drink on cooler days.
   - For busy mornings, prepare your wheatgrass drink or smoothie the night before and store it in a sealed container in the fridge.

4. **Goal for These Days**

   By now, you've likely found a rhythm that works for you. Whether you prefer shots, smoothies, or powdered mixes, the focus is on maintaining consistency. Pay attention to how your body feels and adjust your routine if needed.

5. **Pro Tips for Final Days**
   - Celebrate small wins! Whether it's noticing a boost in energy or feeling more focused,

rewarding yourself for sticking with the plan can help build a lasting habit.
- Track your experience in a journal. Write down how you feel each day to identify what timing, dosage, or preparation method works best for you.

By the end of this 7-day plan, you'll have a good idea of how wheatgrass fits into your lifestyle. Whether you decide to continue with daily use or scale back to a few times a week, you'll be well on your way to reaping the many health benefits wheatgrass has to offer!

When to Take Wheatgrass

Morning:
- Benefits your body by jumpstarting detoxification on an empty stomach.
- Provides a natural energy boost to start the day.

Afternoon:
- Ideal for shaking off the midday slump or replenishing post-workout energy.
- A good option if mornings feel too rushed.

Avoid taking wheatgrass in the evening, as the natural energy boost may interfere with your sleep.

How Much to Start With (and How to Titrate Up)

For beginners, it's important to start small and increase gradually:

- *Day 1–2*: Begin with ½ ounce or ½ teaspoon daily.
- *Day 3–4*: Increase to 1 ounce or 1 teaspoon daily if you feel comfortable.
- *Day 5–7*: If your body tolerates it well, you can take up to 1 ounce twice a day (morning and afternoon).

Note: If you experience mild detox symptoms like fatigue or headaches, slow down your intake and stay hydrated.

Journaling How You Feel

Tracking your experience throughout the week helps you understand your body's response to wheatgrass. Here's what to note in your journal:

- *Energy Levels*: Did you notice any changes in your energy during the day?
- *Digestion*: Has your digestion improved or changed?
- *Mood*: Are there noticeable shifts in how you feel overall?
- *Taste Preferences*: Which methods and add-ins did you enjoy the most?

Pro Tip: Use your journal to plan adjustments for the following week, whether it's changing your dose, trying new add-ins, or switching your timing.

Your 7-day starter plan isn't just about creating a new habit; it's about finding a way to make wheatgrass work for you. Start small, experiment with recipes and timing, and tune into how your body responds. By the end of the week, wheatgrass will feel like a natural part of your routine.

Meal Planning Around Wheatgrass

Integrating wheatgrass into your daily routine is a fantastic step toward better health, but pairing it with the right meals and habits can maximize its benefits. Because wheatgrass is detoxifying and nutrient-dense, your overall diet should be light, nourishing, and supportive of digestion. Here's how to plan your meals and lifestyle around wheatgrass to help you feel your best.

Light, Digestive-Friendly Meals

When you're consuming wheatgrass regularly, choosing meals that are easy on your digestion is key. Wheatgrass works to detoxify the body, so your diet should complement its natural cleansing properties rather than overloading your system. Here are some ideas for meals that are balanced, light, and digestive-friendly:

Breakfast

- *Option 1*: A green smoothie with spinach, banana, almond milk, a teaspoon of wheatgrass powder, and

chia seeds. This is easy to digest and gives you a gentle energy boost.
- *Option 2*: Oatmeal topped with fresh blueberries, ground flaxseeds, and a drizzle of raw honey. Pair with a side of wheatgrass juice for a nutrient-packed start to your day.

Lunch

- *Option 1*: A digestive-friendly Buddha bowl featuring quinoa, roasted sweet potatoes, steamed broccoli, avocado, and a light tahini dressing. This meal is packed with fiber and healthy fats.
- *Option 2*: A simple salad with mixed greens, cucumber, shredded carrots, and grilled chicken or chickpeas. Add a squeeze of lemon for a refreshing flavor boost.

Dinner

- *Option 1*: A warming vegetable soup with carrots, celery, zucchini, and lentils or white beans. Pair it with a slice of whole-grain bread.
- *Option 2*: Grilled fish or tofu with steamed asparagus, brown rice, and a light sprinkle of fresh herbs like parsley or dill.

Snacks
- Fresh fruit like apple slices, orange wedges, or pear slices.
- Raw nuts, like almonds or walnuts, in small portions, to keep energy levels steady.
- Homemade energy bites made with dates, oats, and coconut flakes.

Pro Tip: Avoid heavy, fried, or overly processed meals, as they can weigh down digestion and counteract wheatgrass's cleansing effects.

Hydration Tips

Staying hydrated plays a vital role when incorporating wheatgrass into your routine. Its detoxifying properties can increase the release of toxins, and adequate hydration helps flush them out of your body effectively. Here are some hydration tips to keep in mind:

1. *Start Your Day with Water*: Begin your morning with a glass of warm water and a squeeze of lemon before your wheatgrass shot or smoothie. This helps jumpstart digestion and supports your body's detox process.
2. *Match Water Intake with Wheatgrass*: For every shot (or teaspoon of powdered wheatgrass) you take, aim to drink at least 8–10 ounces of water within the next hour. This prevents dehydration and helps transport nutrients through your system.

3. ***Herbal Teas for Variety***: If plain water feels repetitive, opt for hydrating herbal teas like peppermint, chamomile, or ginger tea. These are soothing to the stomach and can enhance detox effects.
4. ***Add Natural Flavors***: Infuse your water with fruit slices (like cucumber, lemon, or berries) and fresh herbs like mint to encourage you to drink more throughout the day.
5. ***Cut Back on Dehydrating Drinks***: Limit caffeine and alcoholic beverages while detoxing, as they can dehydrate your body and add strain to your liver.

Pro Tip: Monitor your hydration by paying attention to your energy levels, skin, and digestion. Aim for at least 8–10 glasses of water daily, adjusting based on your activity level.

What to Avoid While Detoxing

To make your detox smoother and more effective, there are certain foods and drinks you should avoid. These can make your body work harder to process them and may interfere with the detox process:

1. ***Processed Foods***: Pre-packaged snacks, ready-made meals, and fast food often contain high amounts of salt, sugar, and unhealthy fats. These ingredients can bog down your digestion and slow toxin elimination.

2. ***Sugary Snacks and Desserts***: While tempting, sugary treats can cause energy spikes and crashes, which may leave you feeling tired or sluggish during detox.
3. ***Alcohol***: Alcohol puts extra strain on your liver, which is already working hard to process toxins. Avoid all forms of alcohol during your detox.
4. ***Caffeinated Beverages***: Coffee, soda, and energy drinks can lead to dehydration and affect your gut. If you're a regular coffee drinker, consider switching to decaf or sticking with herbal teas for the duration of the detox.
5. ***Fried and Greasy Foods***: Foods that are fried or heavy with grease can leave you feeling bloated and weigh down your system. Opt for baked, roasted, or steamed dishes instead.

Take a minimalist approach when planning your meals and drinks. Clean, whole food options always work best when paired with wheatgrass.

Wheatgrass Detox Side Effects (and How to Manage Them)

Wheatgrass is often hailed as a superfood, packed with vitamins, minerals, and antioxidants. Many people turn to wheatgrass juice or powder to detoxify their bodies and boost their health. However, like any natural remedy, it's not uncommon for detox symptoms to appear, especially if you're starting fresh. Understanding what's normal and how to manage these side effects will help you get the most out of your wheatgrass detox experience.

Common Reactions to Wheatgrass Detox

While wheatgrass is highly nutritious, it's potent, and your body might take time to adjust to it. Here are some of the most common side effects people experience during a wheatgrass detox:

1. *Nausea*: This is probably the most reported reaction. Wheatgrass can stimulate the digestive system, and if your stomach isn't used to it, you might feel queasy.

The strong, earthy taste of wheatgrass can also contribute to this feeling.
2. ***Headache***: A headache during detox is usually linked to the body releasing toxins. If your body starts flushing out harmful substances, the sudden change can sometimes trigger discomfort, resulting in a headache.
3. ***Fatigue***: Detox processes can be tiring for your body as it works hard to process and eliminate toxins. Low energy levels during a detox are common, especially in the first few days.

These symptoms are usually mild and temporary. However, understanding the difference between normal detox reactions and signs of a potential issue is crucial.

What's Normal vs. What's Not

It's important to know what your body is telling you as you go through a detox. Here's a breakdown to help you gauge your experience:

- ***Normal Symptoms***: Temporary nausea, mild headaches, feeling tired, light dizziness, or changes in bowel movements. These symptoms are expected as your body adjusts and clears out toxins.
- ***When to Be Concerned***: Severe or prolonged nausea that doesn't go away, extreme headaches, difficulty breathing, a racing heart, or severe stomach pain.

These symptoms could be signs of a bad reaction to wheatgrass or another underlying issue. If you experience anything severe, stop consuming wheatgrass immediately and consult a healthcare professional.

Listening to your body during a detox is key to understanding what's normal and what's not. If you experience severe or prolonged symptoms, stop immediately and seek advice from a healthcare professional.

Tips to Ease Detox Symptoms

If you're experiencing mild detox symptoms, there are several ways to make the process smoother and more comfortable:

1. ***Start Small***: Begin with a small dose of wheatgrass juice or powder and gradually increase it. For instance, try 1 ounce a day and work up to 2 ounces over time. This gives your body time to adjust to the new addition.
2. ***Stay Hydrated***: Drinking plenty of water helps flush toxins more efficiently, reducing symptoms like headaches and fatigue. Aim for at least 8–10 glasses of water per day.
3. ***Pair with Food***: Drinking wheatgrass juice on an empty stomach can sometimes trigger nausea. Try having it with a light snack, such as fruit or a handful of nuts, to make it easier on your stomach.

4. ***Listen to Your Body***: If your body is reacting strongly, slow down or take a break. Detox is not a race, and pushing through severe symptoms could do more harm than good. Adjust your intake until you feel more comfortable.
5. ***Rest When Needed***: Fatigue is your body's way of asking for more rest. Get enough sleep and, if needed, take naps during the day to support your body's recovery.
6. ***Opt for High-Quality Wheatgrass***: Poor-quality wheatgrass may contain contaminants or be less effective. Always choose organic, fresh, or reputable products to avoid unnecessary reactions.

Wheatgrass detox symptoms are a sign your body is adjusting, but it's important to listen to your body and adapt as needed. If severe symptoms occur, consult a doctor. Detoxing should improve your health, and with the right approach, you can safely enjoy the benefits of wheatgrass.

7-Day Day-by-Day Plan for Wheatgrass Detox

Starting a wheatgrass detox can be an excellent step toward improving overall health and well-being. This 7-day plan serves as a simple, practical guide to help individuals ease into consuming wheatgrass, observe its effects, and set a foundation for long-term habits. Each day builds on the last to create a smooth and enjoyable experience.

Day 1: Introduction & First Shot

The first day focuses on familiarizing oneself with wheatgrass. A single serving is recommended to keep things easy on the body. A serving might be 1 ounce of fresh wheatgrass juice or 1 teaspoon of wheatgrass powder mixed with water. This should be consumed on an empty stomach, ideally in the morning.

Day 1 is about observing the body's response. Wheatgrass is potent, and first-timers might notice mild effects such as a slight boost in energy or unusual digestion. These reactions are the body's way of adapting to the detox. Drinking extra water throughout the day supports the detox process by flushing out toxins.

Day 2: Adding a Second Daily Serving

The second day introduces a second serving of wheatgrass to gradually increase the body's exposure. The first serving in the morning remains the same. A second serving is added during the afternoon or early evening, but not too late to avoid an energy spike before bedtime.

This gradual step allows time to gauge how the extra serving feels in the body. The approach minimizes overwhelming side effects, especially for individuals with sensitive stomachs. Keeping meals light and nutritious also aids the detox.

Day 3: Incorporating into a Smoothie

On Day 3, a creative twist is introduced by blending wheatgrass into a smoothie. This keeps things exciting while masking the earthy flavor of wheatgrass for those who may find it unpleasant.

A simple recipe could include wheatgrass, a banana, some spinach or kale, frozen berries, and a dairy-free milk like almond or oat milk. The smoothie provides a nutrient-packed breakfast or snack while helping the stomach handle wheatgrass more easily. Adding natural ingredients ensures the smoothie remains detox-friendly.

Day 4: Tracking Energy & Digestion

Midway through the plan, Day 4 encourages individuals to reflect on the changes they're noticing. They might observe differences in their energy levels, gut health, or even clearer skin. A journal can be helpful for tracking how they feel physically and emotionally since starting the detox.

Additionally, this day offers a chance to adjust intake if needed. For instance, if there are any persistent discomforts, reducing back to one daily serving might be a better fit for the body. Staying hydrated and maintaining gentle, balanced meals are critical at this stage.

Day 5: Trying a New Recipe

Day 5 shakes up the routine by encouraging the exploration of a new recipe using wheatgrass. This might be a fresh juice blend featuring ingredients like carrots, apples, and ginger to create a delicious, nutritious drink.

Adding variety keeps the detox exciting and prevents monotony. It also offers a chance to experiment with flavor combinations that enhance the wheatgrass experience while sticking to healthy, detox-friendly ingredients.

Day 6: Reflecting on Changes

By Day 6, the benefits of the detox often start to shine through. Individuals are likely noticing increased energy, improved digestion, or even a stronger sense of focus. Reflecting on these positive changes can be motivating.

This is also a time to celebrate reaching this stage of the detox. Tracking progress from Day 1 helps to solidify any good habits developed along the way. The goal is to recognize small victories and keep building momentum.

Day 7: Wrap-Up and Next Steps

Day 7 marks the final step of the detox. It is an opportunity to assess the overall experience and decide how to move forward. Individuals can think about whether they want to make wheatgrass a permanent part of their diet or simply incorporate it periodically.

Planning healthy habits beyond the detox ensures lasting health benefits. Setting an intention to maintain a balanced diet, stay hydrated, and prioritize rest enables the body to thrive. Many may choose to continue daily wheatgrass servings or use it intermittently as a nutritional boost.

A 7-day wheatgrass detox offers a great way to explore its benefits while introducing healthy habits. By taking it one day at a time, individuals can maximize the positive effects without overwhelming their bodies. Thoughtful planning, listening to feedback, and a willingness to adapt ensure a smooth, rewarding detox experience. With this structured approach, wheatgrass can become a valuable ally in supporting long-term health and well-being.

How to Continue After 7 Days

After your initial 7-day introduction to wheatgrass, the next step is to build a sustainable routine that aligns with your health and wellness goals. Wheatgrass offers immense benefits when consumed regularly, but maintaining balance and tuning into your body is essential for lasting success. Here's how to move forward confidently.

Building a Long-Term Routine

Consistency is key when it comes to reaping the benefits of wheatgrass. Whether you continue daily or scale back to a few times a week, the goal is to make consumption a manageable and enjoyable part of your lifestyle.

1. **Tips for Establishing a Routine:**
    - ***Start with a Schedule***: Decide how often wheatgrass fits into your week. Many find that 1 ounce daily or 3–5 times a week is ideal for sustained energy and overall wellness.
    - ***Choose a Time of Day***: Morning is a popular choice because wheatgrass juice can boost

energy and kickstart the metabolism. Schedule it alongside regular habits, like breakfast or your morning cup of tea, to integrate it seamlessly into your day.

- ***Prepare in Advance***: Growing wheatgrass at home? Keep multiple trays staggered so there's always a fresh batch ready. If you're juicing on the go, prep fresh juice in advance and freeze extra servings in small, convenient portions, like ice cube trays.

2. **Keep It Interesting:**

Sticking with the same routine can get repetitive, so experiment to keep things fresh.

- ***Explore Recipes***: Mix wheatgrass with your favorite ingredients to customize the flavor. Try smoothie bowls with frozen fruits or combine wheatgrass juice with herbal teas for a unique twist.
- ***Combine with Other Superfoods***: Pair wheatgrass with health-boosting ingredients like spirulina, matcha, or chia seeds. A wheatgrass shot before a turmeric latte, for example, can offer complementary benefits.
- ***Experiment with Methods***: While shots are the most common way to consume wheatgrass, you can use powdered wheatgrass for variety. Stir it

into soups, salad dressings, or even homemade energy bars.

3. **Stay Accountable:**
   - *Set Goals*: Whether it's improving digestion or boosting immunity, align wheatgrass consumption with your health priorities.
   - *Track Progress*: Keep journaling how wheatgrass affects your energy, mood, digestion, and skin. Reflecting on your improvements can reinforce motivation and make the habit stick.

By building wheatgrass into your routine and keeping it versatile, this superfood can become a natural part of your long-term health plan.

When to Take Breaks

While wheatgrass is packed with nutrients, taking occasional breaks is beneficial for giving your body time to reset and ensuring long-term balance.

Why Breaks Are Important:
- *Prevent Overexposure*: Even superfoods can become too much if consumed without pause. Over-consuming wheatgrass for extended periods may risk nutrient buildup or reduce its effectiveness over time.

- ***Encourage Variety***: Breaks allow you to diversify your diet with other nutrient sources, ensuring your body receives a broad spectrum of vitamins and minerals.
- ***Reduce Adaptation***: Your system can become accustomed to regular wheatgrass consumption. Taking breaks can help prevent your body from plateauing, so it remains responsive to its benefits.

When to Take a Break:

- If you notice diminishing effects, like less energy or changes in digestion, it might be time for a short pause.
- If detox symptoms, like fatigue or mild nausea, persist after several weeks of use, your body could need a reset.
- Seasonal breaks can also be a great way to cycle wheatgrass into your lifestyle. For instance, take it consistently during spring and summer and pause during autumn to focus on other health practices.

How to Pause and Restart:

- Gradually reduce your intake over a week before stopping. For example, taper from daily doses to 3 times a week, then 1, and eventually take a complete break for 2–4 weeks.
- When reintroducing wheatgrass, start with smaller amounts like ½ ounce and slowly increase toward your

preferred daily serving. Your body will likely respond positively after the pause.

Taking breaks ensures you avoid over-reliance on wheatgrass while maintaining its effectiveness over time.

Listening to Your Body's Feedback

Every person's body is unique, and what works for others might not always be ideal for you. Wheatgrass is powerful, and the key to optimizing its benefits lies in paying close attention to how your body reacts.

1. **Monitoring Physical Responses:**
   - *Energy*: Do you feel more energized when you take wheatgrass in the morning or during an afternoon slump? If you notice energy dips, consider adjusting the timing of your intake.
   - *Digestion*: Improved digestion is a sign that your dosage might be just right. However, bloating or discomfort may signal the need to cut back or take it less frequently.
   - *Skin and Hair*: Many notice clearer skin, faster hair growth, and a healthy glow after regular use. If these changes occur, it's a good indication that wheatgrass is supporting your overall wellness.

2. **Tracking Emotional and Mental Well-Being:**
   - Clarity and Focus: Wheatgrass is packed with nutrients that may impact cognitive function. Pay attention to moments of heightened focus or clarity and make note of when they occur.
   - Mood Swings or Fatigue: If emotional shifts arise, especially fatigue or irritability, check if you're coupling wheatgrass with lighter meals and sufficient hydration. Heavy foods during detox can sometimes heighten these symptoms.
3. **Adjusting Dosage Based on Feedback:**
   - Start small and work your way up to your ideal serving size. For instance, if 1 ounce feels too strong, reduce to ½ ounce every other day and build to 1 full ounce gradually.
   - If you feel your body is thriving, you can experiment with slightly larger doses (up to 2 ounces per session), but monitor for any side effects like nausea or headaches.

Some people prefer wheatgrass shots while others enjoy blending it into morning routines. Try different methods, like pairing it with apple juice for a sweeter flavor or using green powder in recipes if juicing feels time-consuming.

Keep in mind that your body's needs may shift over time due to seasons, lifestyle changes, or personal health goals. Staying flexible is the secret to a long-term relationship with wheatgrass.

By building a tailored routine, taking mindful breaks, and tuning in to your body's unique feedback, wheatgrass can remain a pillar of your wellness practices. Whether consumed for its detoxifying properties, energy-boosting nutrients, or overall vitality, making wheatgrass a sustainable part of your lifestyle helps you enjoy its full range of benefits.

Conclusion

Wheatgrass is more than just a vibrant green plant; it's a powerful ally in your wellness journey. By now, you've seen its versatility, unmatched nutrient profile, and the many ways it can transform your health. From detoxifying your body and boosting your energy to improving your skin and digestion, wheatgrass has proven itself as an accessible, natural superfood with benefits for nearly every aspect of your life.

Integrating wheatgrass into your daily routine doesn't have to be complicated. Whether you prefer taking a quick and concentrated wheatgrass shot or blending it into a smoothie with your favorite fruits, there are countless ways to make it work for your taste and lifestyle. For those who enjoy growing their own, planting and harvesting wheatgrass at home offers unbeatable freshness and satisfaction. And if you're short on time, reputable pre-made juices or powdered forms provide convenient alternatives without sacrificing quality.

What's most important is finding an approach that feels natural and sustainable for you. Start small by incorporating wheatgrass into a morning shot, a mid-afternoon smoothie, or a post-workout recovery shake. Pair it with other superfoods like matcha, chia seeds, or turmeric to further amplify the benefits and keep your routine exciting. And if you share your home with family, consider introducing wheatgrass to your kids or even your pets for a full-circle wellness win.

You've also learned how to tune into your body's needs during this process. Starting with a small dose, staying hydrated, and paying attention to how your body reacts will help you unlock the full potential of wheatgrass while avoiding any discomfort. Remember, balance is key. If you need a break, take one, and when you return to wheatgrass, your body will welcome its revitalizing properties all over again.

Thank you for taking the time to explore this guide and for investing in your health. It's not always easy to try something new, but your curiosity and willingness to learn are the first steps to lasting change. By incorporating wheatgrass into your routine, you're not just adding a healthy habit; you're choosing to nourish yourself from the inside out with a truly remarkable superfood.

Now, it's time to take action. Start small with a dose, a recipe, or even by growing your own wheatgrass at home. Share this newfound knowledge with loved ones and encourage them to join you in exploring the benefits. Every positive step you take toward wellness matters, and wheatgrass is an easy, impactful way to make a difference in how you feel every day.

FAQs

How should I start the 7-day wheatgrass detox?

Start with a small serving on Day 1, such as 1 ounce of wheatgrass juice or 1 teaspoon of powder mixed with water. Drink it on an empty stomach, ideally in the morning. Gradually increase servings as suggested in the day-by-day guide while listening to your body's responses.

What if I don't like the taste of wheatgrass?

If the taste is too strong, try adding wheatgrass to a smoothie on Day 3. Blend it with fruits like banana or berries and a liquid base such as almond milk to mask the flavor while still getting the benefits.

Are there any side effects I should expect during the detox?

Common side effects include mild nausea, headaches, or fatigue, especially during the first few days. These are normal and usually caused by the body adjusting and releasing toxins. Stay hydrated and eat light, healthy meals to ease these symptoms.

Can I drink more than two servings of wheatgrass in a day?

Two servings per day are plenty for beginners. Once the body adjusts, some people may increase to 3 servings, but it's important not to overdo it. Too much wheatgrass can cause digestive discomfort. Listen to your body and adjust as needed.

What foods should I eat during the 7-day wheatgrass detox?

Pair wheatgrass with light, digestive-friendly meals like soups, salads, steamed vegetables, and fresh fruits. Avoid processed foods, sugary snacks, alcohol, and caffeine, as these can disrupt the detox process.

How will I know if the detox is working?

Signs of progress include increased energy, improved digestion, clearer skin, and better focus. It's also helpful to keep a journal to track how your body feels throughout the week.

Can I continue the detox beyond 7 days?

Yes, you can make wheatgrass part of your regular routine. After the detox, continue with 1–2 servings daily or incorporate it into your diet periodically as a boost. Remember to take breaks if you feel any discomfort or fatigue.

References and Helpful Links

Cronkleton, E. (2024, September 23). Wheatgrass benefits: 8 reasons to enjoy. Healthline.
https://www.healthline.com/health/food-nutrition/wheatgrass-benefits

Swasthi. (2022, March 4). Wheatgrass shot. Swasthi's Recipes.
https://www.indianhealthyrecipes.com/wheatgrass-shot-recipe/

Pellegrini, A. (2023, August 22). 7 Ways to Sneak Wheatgrass into Recipes. Navitas Organics.
https://navitasorganics.com/blogs/navitaslife/7-ways-to-sneak-wheatgrass-into-recipes?srsltid=AfmBOooxYZzHG8ReTFQwZWQCtOXnhym6ABH_h3-rRZ0kC9CahDRNM3p3

Beverages, H. (2023, June 20). Best time to drink wheatgrass juice to get benefits (with recipe, side effects and cost). Hugg Beverages.
https://gethugg.com/blog/best-time-to-drink-wheatgrass-juice/

True Leaf Market. (2012, October 18). True Leaf Market Seed Company | Buy Non-GMO, Heirloom, Organic seeds.
https://trueleafmarket.com/blogs/articles/how-much-wheatgrass-juice-to-drink?srsltid=AfmBOopHX4jcaoqyml1izRHNMTfWxpqkp964H0Ob92t0XM_JXcFOzpwG

Ld, L. D. R. (2024, October 15). How wheatgrass can Transform your health: 11 Key Benefits. Verywell Health.
https://www.verywellhealth.com/wheatgrass-benefits-8720193

www.ingramcontent.com/pod-product-compliance
Lightning Source LLC
LaVergne TN
LVHW012031060526
838201LV00061B/4556